BIRDS
OF THE MIDWEST

poems by

Jane Hufford Downes

Finishing Line Press
Georgetown, Kentucky

BIRDS
OF THE MIDWEST

Publisher: Leah Huete de Maines
Editor: Christen Kincaid
Cover Art: Debbie Salsbury Dietrick
Author Photo: Sue McCormick Kearns
Cover Design: Elizabeth Maines McCleavy

Order online: www.finishinglinepress.com
also available on amazon.com

Author inquiries and mail orders:
Finishing Line Press
PO Box 1626
Georgetown, Kentucky 40324
USA

Table of Contents

In loving memory of Sylvia K. Salsbury,
ever grateful for her abundant friendship.
Her encouragement gave my poetry wings.

BIRDING FROM A WHEELCHAIR AT ELM CREEK

After Li Bai's "Gazing at a Waterfall on Mount Lu"

Warblers stitch treetops to the heavens,
their song, a dizi flute, trills bright and high.
Below, my wheels mud-bound to Earth,
under an oak with roots spread wide.
The flavor of lost freedom is a bitter
melon, weedy and astringent. Between
budding branches, I pursue them,
watch each bird's buoyant movement as it flies.
My binoculars capture their banners, as my
heart struggles, overwhelmed by joy, by sorrow.

"Heavens High, Earth wide.
Bitter between them flies my sorrow."

PERCEPTIONS

For every color we perceive, birds can see multiple
distinct colors. Relative to birds, we humans are color-blind.
            —*Scott Lanyon, Professor of Ecology, Evolution,*
            and Behavior

The life of a bird may be brief,
but there is compensation: the ability
to soar, and a glorious world of color,
unimagined by any human eye.
Is it any wonder Chagall dreamed of flying,
Monet's skies quivered with light,
Van Gogh adored the heavens?
They had the souls of birds,
trapped in human bodies,
trying to get their eyes back.

MOURNING DOVE

Dawn in Ohio. The soft gray dove
flies up from underneath the spruce,
a whisper of wings, to a low branch. She surveys
the growing light with piercing eyes,
and calmly provides a cooing,
calling lament, intensifying
the stillness. Tranquility settles
on the mist in layers. Quiet. She swoops
to walk among the grasses and dust
at the edge of the garden, calm
in the long shadows, while the sun rises.
As we hurry through this new day,
may some measure of sure serenity
fluff its feathers near our hearts
while peace settles in layers like mist.

CROW SONG

The nursery rhyme, One for Sorrow, was first published in 1780, attributed to Mother Goose. It is incorporated here in italics.

One for sorrow. Restless lone crow,
an ominous predictor. Spirit messenger,
poet thief: his glossy feathers
vibrate with questions and troubles.

Two for mirth. Breaking into raucous laughter from the power line
above the alley,
they recognize friendly faces from yesterday,
gleefully sharing intricate and complex lives.

Three for a wedding. Solemn as priest, in a pine outside the church,
three crows lift suddenly, fly over as lace-frost and crow-suit step
across the doorsill.
Their encircling flight becomes a blessing.

Four for a birth. She is awakened by two pairs of crows.
Listening in the gathering dawn, she wonders
about this crow-child striving to be born, the one with dark eyes
who would sing in a harsh but insistent voice.

Five for silver. For five summers, the one-legged crow
returned to the birdbath with his rowdy family. Back again,
he searches among stones like a miser looking for silver, wary
before drinking, then flies in a long arc above the garden, gone.

Six for gold. As wheat turns gold in the field
six crows gather in widening circles of peace,
knowing that today they'll get all they desire
before the harsh scarcities of winter set in.

Seven for a secret not to be told. Gregarious
crows share constant conversation among
themselves, yet share so little of their wisdom
and understanding with us tall featherless birds.

Eight for heaven. Crows colonize the edges
of our daily lives, unnoticed unless we're startled
by brash voices overhead, a beckoning.
Heaven is found on earth in unlikely places.

Nine for hell. Gathering to sing in the dead of night,
with lyrical harshness of broken wings, sunken eyes,
and nightmare struggle. They wait, blameless, trying
to escape sinister expectations and the smell of death.

Ten for the devil's own to tell. A murder of crows
gathers in a circle on brittle grass, squawking loudly.
Mourning ruffled black death. Uneasy. Solemn. Magical
prophets, fallen angels, messengers of gods.

BABY

He'll grow to be a noble bird, with a proud crest
and rich red plumage, bringing elegant hope
to the snow-covered lilac bush in February. Yet today
he is a gawky fledgling, all feet and scruffy feathers.
Every schoolchild knows the brilliant redbird—
he'll certainly have a reputation to live up to.
But for now, this little one has much to learn
in a world full of confounding things. With
just barely enough feathers to leave the nest,
he flew, brave and impetuous. How to get
into trouble comes naturally for some.
His mother calls *what-cheer, what-cheer,*
while he stands awkward and fierce,
ready to take on the world, as soon as he figures out
how to get out of the window well.

NOVEMBER MIGRATION:
SHERBURNE NATIONAL WILDLIFE REFUGE

Water nearly frozen now, the surface has the luster
of pewter, of a shadow in moonlight. Ice forms
at the margins, gathering around each sepia reed
poking above the surface. Snow drifts down
from felted clouds. A drowsy edge of dawn
offers no warmth to sleeping birds. Sandhill Crane
wakes slowly, stretching, shaking one foot
and then the other, dislodging shards of ice
accumulated overnight. Standing ankle-deep
in bitter water, she hears a faint, compelling voice
calling from southern places. Will today
be the day to flex her stiffened toes, gather
awkward wings, and leave this frozen realm behind?
She offers a harsh prayer, hurls herself into the wind,
follows the familiar path of her keening ancestors.

GRAVES

Mostly dead birds, a pet turtle, and once
a road-killed squirrel. We played at grief,
buried our scavenged dead in sandy earth
under the oak tree. Prayers offered up
to the god of small children over graves
marked with crossed popsicle sticks
and outlined with stones. Sometimes
there were violets or dandelions.
Visiting my mother's graveside, a lifetime later,
red-winged blackbirds and whippoorwills call
while lilacs wilt in the sun.
I think of hollow bird bones,
stones weighing them down, and
my mother, finally flying.

TEACHING BIRDS TO SING

Along the Maumee River, ancestors and grandmothers repeat
stories of blossoms and beginnings, telling
of the Great Mother teaching birds to sing:
gently, sweetly. Saying—listen to the Silence
until music resonates in your bones.
Your task, this soft April morning,
is as simple as teaching birds to sing.
You may feel inadequate for the job,
but you are primed, ready to burst forth
with the melodies of your heart. All you need
is to stand on your own two feet, go deeply
into Silence, and you will know the hymn.
Offer your song, quavering and pure,
as white petals drift from apple trees.

SINGING ELVIS TO THE CHICKENS

Aunt Doris strides among the constant scuffle and flutter, calm
as an angel on a mission, singing Elvis to the chickens—pure notes
of "Earth Angel" and "Can't Help Falling in Love"
float with bits of feather on slanted sunlight.
The smell of ammonia tickles, tastes of dust and alfalfa
at the back of the throat. The chickens offer
a backup choir warm and companionable as sunlight.
Gallus Gallus Domesticus.
The sun crosses the sky to get to the other side,
each moment an egg gathered in the apron pockets of time.
Domesticated sun, flying awkwardly over Fulton County, Ohio,
illuminates a fallen feather, like a message from an angel.

RESURRECTION

Light replenishes the woods,
bathes tree trunks, touches
newly green shoots of daffodils.
It is suddenly full day, past the point
when the sun lifts over the horizon
in blessing. A time for renewal, as birds,
weary from long journeys, prepare
to start again. Singing songs,
building nests, accepting resurrection.
Returning season after season
to the same sheltering branches,
carrying spring on their relentless wings.

SHELTERING—MARCH

Spring started, with its migrations and longings,
its joys and disquiet. We welcomed flashes of purple crocus,
demure snowdrops, robins calling from the spruce, hellebore
bowing in prayer under evergreen leaves. Then
overnight, a dusting of snow covered everything.
Now the cardinals take turns at the feeder, uneasy.
A grackle, mysterious as night, cocks his iridescent head,
followed by a sudden darkness of wings as his 12 companions
jostle for space at the feeder. Each wing shines
like my father's shoes. Footprints sneak
outside the door, left behind by a possum
on his midnight rounds. House finches huddle
on the leeward side of the feeder, with a rosy blush
like the cheeks of children sent to play in the snow.
All is hushed, waiting for the coming storm.
A woodcock, blown off course by the night wind,
hops and bobs along the fence, a balestra before lunging,
his bill a sword probing the snow at his feet.
We wait, putting off leave-taking,
hunkering down for the storm.

37 KINDS OF WARBLERS

On May eleventh, near Oak Harbor, Ohio,
I saw 37 kinds of warblers in a small patch of woods
at Magee Marsh. Cascades of the purest sound
I've ever heard—a liquid burbling like joy
spilling over, more extravagant and well-costumed
than opera at the Met. Each bird a mere half ounce
of wonder and fluff, beating the odds with unimaginable
tenacity, on a migratory path 1500 miles long. Riding
air currents through cool nights, following
rivers and instinct, chasing the northern edge of Spring.

The air smells of last night's rain, and dogwood branches glisten.
Obsessively, we stalk the trails, scan shrubs
and treetops, searching for that telltale bobbing flight,
a small flitting movement caught at the corner of an eye.
Quick punctuations of color flash through the undergrowth –
commas of yellow, russet slashes between small branches.
Blackburnians, Red-eyed Vireos, Black-throated Blues,
Northern Parulas, Ceruleans, and Common yellows.
Gathered together in large numbers, they are
an overwhelming spectacle—each bird part diva,
part insubstantial fairy, part indomitable grit.

Seen through binoculars, their feisty hearts beat
under sleek feathers, their dark eyes shine with purpose.
Life brings unspeakable sadness, daily threats. Yet
in the balance, the grace of 37 kinds of warblers,
permanently tips the cosmic scales
toward mercy, that single day in May.

HOLLOW BONES

Fragile in their hollow bones fledglings pause
on the edge of the nest.
Strength of feather and melody
soon determine flight.
Young birds ask questions
with eager eyes: are we
strong enough
to fly? From the trees
a clear note resonates
close to the bone: strong enough,
strong enough to fly.

PIPING PLOVER

*The sum total of everything we know about animals is just about
equal to the sum total of everything we don't know. That's why
we continue to explore the mysteries of the Wild Kingdom.*
—Marlin Perkins

Piping plovers are wind-up toys darting along the beach.
Their long stick legs scissor at the edge
of childhood memories, scrapbook days
along Lake Erie, with the zing of ozone
promising summer rain. A melancholy whistle
spools out across the wavelets lapping the shore.
Charadrius melodus. Rain singer.
In a slight basin carved into soft dry sand, three
tiny eggs so well camouflaged they're barely there.
I bend over and watch carefully, but nothing happens.
Longing for the excitement of my own real-life
Mutual of Omaha moment, I wish for a wise
overvoice explanation. Someday I'll become
Marlin Perkins, with a camera and an eye for wonder.

I figure I should practice being observant, and try
to grow a mustache. Up and down the beach, I search
like a plover—run and pause, run and pause,
tender feet chasing the shore birds of destiny.
Decades pass, and Lake Erie still nibbles away
at the shoreline in the eternal battle between
land and water. Quiet rain rolls in across
gray waves, and plovers run along the shore,
looking for sandy places to lay unseen eggs.

HUMMINGBIRD

Sitting under oak trees, in quiet
conversation, we speak of everything
and nothing, like old friends
or new lovers. Darting above the azalea,
a thousand facets of metallic light appear
at the edge of vision. The hummingbird
floats on our breath, on our murmured words,
on the scent of Coral Bells and Bee Balm. Glittering,
it approaches an open flower, is accepted
by its shape, its blush of color. The minute bird,
all focused energy and compressed desire,
receives offerings, moves on; carving space
into curves within curves. Time hovers
above blossoms, floating on wind and whirring wings.
Abruptly, the hummingbird leaves us in startled silence,
wondering if we're the ones suddenly moving
backward, reckless and uncontrolled.

WHEELING WINGS

Hope is the thing with feathers.
—Emily Dickinson

Seasons wheel slowly, ready
for the next step that doesn't come
without pain. Things change, sometimes
even for the better. Migration happens
over and over as seasons turn. Earthbound,
boundaries firmly established, I notice
the lift of wings, lilting calls in nesting season,
a flash of color between the leaves. Above the river,
an eagle rides the thermals, belonging to wind and sky,
muscular and effortless. Below, a warbler struggles,
flies into the wind in fits and starts, lands, clinging
to a twig. Singing wonder into the sky, he takes
Emily Dickinson to heart. Nature only asks
that we love by paying attention: the changing light,
a loon's persistent call, wheels turning on the trail.
Pure moments of awe, encompassing love
within each moment—this is hope, that thing with feathers.

IMPROBABILITIES

Bats hear shapes, see with their ears, navigate
without light. Their ultrasonic echolocation is precise.
Do they see colors as echoed textures?

Trees eat air, rising from carbon dioxide.
During photosynthesis, their massive trunks,
delicate leaves, and acorns pulled out of the sky.

Honeybees dance maps, wiggling in patterns
for distance and angle, precise communication so others
know where the flowers are. What else is in their vocabulary?

Small birds fly across oceans to other hemispheres, trusting
memories of their own, and of their ancestors, a vast understanding
of atmospheric conditions, geography, and determination.

Looking at the absurd beauty of the world, its precise particularities,
we are astonished. Improbable things happen all around us, wonder
upon wonder, a complex puzzle, understood dimly.

BIRDWATCHING

I used to believe that birds sang because they were happy.
Happy because they could fly. Youth seldom looks closely
at what it loves. Not by accident is bird-watching
a mostly gray-haired hobby. The skill to enter silence
is an acquired one, taking time we once thought
we didn't have. On a May morning, when the air
aches sweet as buttercream and twigs burst
into leaf, it's all trills and callings, chitterings and chirpings,
counterpoint and staking claim—and lusting, lusting, lusting.
Compelled by life force and inborn longing, who
would consider the need to be happy? Still, I like to think
flying gives them a lift, that their spirits soar
along with their feathers and bones.

WINTER SOLSTICE

The Moon drops one or two feathers into the field.
—James Wright

The owl flies silently under the small cold moon,
her shadow gliding dark across the field. Snow
glimmers quicksilver, platinum.

In between dried grasses a small rustling
and the scent of fear. Shadows
as long as the night cower in the bitter cold.

A mouse trembles in the dark—
there is no comfort here. Like a capricious wind,
the owl moves on. Provisional salvation

in this singular moment, for this one small life.
A feather drifts to earth,
as if the moon has messages to tell.

DINOSAUR FEATHERS

It's important that people understand dinosaurs are still among us. They're represented by at least 13,000 species alive today."
—Mark Norell, Chair of Paleontology, American Museum of Natural History

Before yesterday,
the right rock hadn't
been overturned.
Some pterosaurs were
flapping wings all through
the Mesozoic era. Pterodactyls
with hollow bones and feathers,
and giraffe-birds, browsing
in treetops, scanned horizons
with their melancholy eyes.
Raven-sized Archaeopteryx
had wings, flight feathers,
sharp teeth. They flew toward
the future, imperceptibly transforming
into Blackburnian Warblers,
leaving their memoirs
written in bone, stone, and feathers.

LIFT

Poised, forever liminal, at the edge
of something primal—enduring earth,
the restless vastness of the sea, the sky
that itself is the edge of the swirling chaos
of uncountable stars. Gull poised at the center
of everything. Feeling the support of solid rock
underfoot, the swell of waves, the rush
of moving air. Knowing the galaxies within
a single drop of water. This wingtip is the center
of the immense intensity of the universe, of vast
light years colliding in a brief moment. We grasp
the intricacy of life, its subtle powerful beauty. Then,
that soaring feeling: a prayer of elation and humility,
as the gull, with one flap of her strong wings, lifts to the sky.

TAKING FLIGHT

The world is mystical, endearing. Life
cycles round, a child's top spinning.
Moon ebbs and flows. We have
all time. On some future day, I will return.
A particle of dust becoming prairie,
in the whispering breeze, nurturing clover
which feeds the buzz and lift
of a bumblebee, and who, in turn, becomes
lunch for a crow. Stars dance and reel.
The music of the spheres plays on.

In some distant future, dreams realized,
a molecule will learn to fly,
a smidgen of immortality.

TUNDRA SWANS

The swans are insubstantial as snow, disappearing
when they touch the surface of the frozen lake,
melting into yielding whiteness.
Wings whisper in cold bright air.
They taste metal and tannin of cold,
remember the faint scent of running water,
like music, drifting toward dreams. Odette
arrives from Nicollet, Minnesota, in a down parka
and Sorel® boots, a woman at the center
of a snowflake swarm. She resists
harsh blizzards of loneliness,
flies with swans and dances a *Pas de Deux*
with the Northwind. A brutal winter brings a mild spring.
White lilacs will bloom, and voices of a phantom home
will beckon. The swans rise into fog and flurry,
speaking harsh assurances, and, laughing,
disappear into white canvas sky.

PROPHECY

The crabapple tree sings to the robins in winter,
while ice-glazed branches click together like
pearls tossed on a hardwood floor. Rust and gray shagbark
scant armor for the onslaught of 27 below.
The flock of robins stayed through winter,
returning each day to the crabtree, intoxicated
by the fermented tang of the last few shriveled apples,
surviving another day, smelling the warmth of August under the
    snow.
Hopkins, Minnesota, seems an unlikely place for robins to
    overwinter,
yet here they are, fluffing their feathers and chatting amongst
    themselves
as if survival isn't risky, as if their name isn't Turdus migratorius,
as if they've never heard of Florida, the Promised Land
where earthworms are plentiful and sunlight golden.
Today the sky is the soft gray of an approaching snowstorm,
fourteen inches predicted. Yet the eagles are rearranging sticks
in their nest by the river; eggtime is coming.
The confused robins of prophecy, predicting spring every day
through five months of blizzard and record low temperatures
will finally, eventually, be right. They will endure
until the crabapple tree bursts into pink, its branches
sheltering sky-colored eggs in a nest of mud and grass.

Jane **Hufford Downes** is a poet and writer, an avid birder, and the author of the poetry collection *Birds of the Midwest.*

A few years ago, Jane started using a wheelchair. Besides the obvious challenges, it opened up a whole new world. Hitting the trails in her wheelchair, she traveled more slowly, looked up, and was soon an avid birder.

While birding is a new interest, writing is a lifelong passion. Jane worked as an architectural writer and editor, and as a freelance writer. Publishing credits include articles, poetry, essays, and fiction. Jane enjoys teaching workshops in poetry and writing. She studied writing at the University of Toledo and currently studies poetry at The Loft Literary Center in Minneapolis. Previous poetry collections include *What I Assume and Notes Between Friends.*

Jane was awarded first place for the Florence Hynes Willette Award for Humor in Poetry (2019) and placed first in the Southern MN Poets Society contest for Narrative Poetry (2020). Her first published poem appeared in Good Housekeeping Magazine. Jane was awarded the Grand Prize for Ekphrasis Poetry by The Toledo Arts Commission and received awards from the League of Minnesota Poets in each of the last four years.

When not writing or birding, Jane enjoys jazz and symphonic music, especially concerts in Twin Cities parks, where music is often accompanied by birdsong. Concerned about climate change, she actively promotes sustainability, and participates in local environmental initiatives centered on water quality. An avid reader, she is active in community writing and literacy activities, including volunteering as a tutor in an Adult ESL/GED program. Jane's family includes her husband of forty-four years, a daughter and son-in-law, and four of the most exceptional red-haired grandchildren on the planet. She has lived in Ohio and Michigan, and currently calls Hopkins, Minnesota, home.